J BIO COLUMBUS
Schaefer, Lola M., 1950-
Christopher Columbus /

# Christopher Columbus

by Lola M. Schaefer

Consulting Editor: Gail Saunders-Smith, Ph.D.
Content Consultant: Beverly McMillan,
The Mariners' Museum
Newport News, Virginia

## Pebble Books

an imprint of Capstone Press
Mankato, Minnesota

Pebble Books are published by Capstone Press
151 Good Counsel Drive, P.O. Box 669, Mankato, Minnesota 56002
http://www.capstone-press.com

2  3  4  5  6  07  06  05  04  03  02

*Library of Congress Cataloging-in-Publication Data*
Schaefer, Lola M., 1950–
    Christopher Columbus / by Lola M. Schaefer.
    p. cm.—(First biographies)
    Includes bibliographical references and index.
    Summary: Simple text and photographs introduce the life of the Italian explorer
who sailed to America in 1492.
    ISBN-13: 978-0-7368-1173-6 (hardcover)
    ISBN-10: 0-7368-1173-7 (hardcover)
    ISBN-13 978-0-7368-9368-8 (softcover pbk.)
    ISBN-10: 0-7368-9368-7 (softcover pbk.)
    1. Columbus, Christopher—Juvenile literature. 2. Explorers—America—
Biography—Juvenile literature. 3. Explorers—Spain—Biography—Juvenile literature.
4. America—Discovery and exploration—Spanish—Juvenile literature.
[1. Columbus, Christopher. 2. Explorers. 3. America—Discovery and exploration—
Spanish.] I. Title. II. Series: First biographies (Mankato, Minn.)
E111 .S32 2002
970.01′5′092—dc21                                                    2001004832

# Note to Parents and Teachers

The First Biographies series supports national history standards for
units on people and culture. This book describes and illustrates the life
of Christopher Columbus. The photographs support early readers in
understanding the text. This book also introduces early readers to
subject-specific vocabulary words, which are defined in the Words to
Know section. Early readers may need assistance to read some words
and to use the Table of Contents, Words to Know, Read More, Internet
Sites, and Index/Word List sections of the book.

# Table of Contents

## Time Line

1451
born

4

Christopher Columbus was born in Italy in 1451. His father was a weaver. Christopher made cloth in his father's shop. But he dreamed about sailing on the seas.

## Time Line

1451
born

around 1480
makes voyages
to sell cloth

Christopher's father knew his son loved the sea. He asked Christopher to sell their cloth in faraway places. Christopher learned how to sail large ships.

## Time Line

1451
born

around 1480
makes voyages
to sell cloth

Christopher became a good sailor. He read charts and maps. He kept the ships on course by following the stars.

Europe    Asia

## Time Line

1451
born

around 1480
makes voyages
to sell cloth

1484
first explains his
idea to sail west
to reach Asia

10

Sailors had always traveled east from Europe. They sailed to the rich cities of Asia. But Christopher wanted to try sailing west. He talked about finding a new course to Asia.

## Time Line

1451
born

around 1480
makes voyages
to sell cloth

1484
first explains his
idea to sail west
to reach Asia

Christopher also worked as a mapmaker for his brother. He met great sailors and thinkers. They knew the sea and faraway lands. They thought Christopher's idea could work.

## Time Line

| 1451 born | around 1480 makes voyages to sell cloth | 1484 first explains his idea to sail west to reach Asia | 1486 asks queen of Spain for help |

Christopher asked the kings
and queens of many countries
for money. Some said the
trip would cost too much.
Others said sailing west
to Asia would not work.

◀ Christopher talking to the queen of Spain

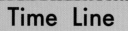

## Time Line

| 1451 born | around 1480 makes voyages to sell cloth | 1484 first explains his idea to sail west to reach Asia | 1486 asks queen of Spain for help |

Finally, the queen of Spain agreed to help Christopher. She gave him a crew, food, money, and three ships. The ships were the *Niña*, the *Pinta*, and the *Santa Maria*.

◀ the *Niña*, the *Pinta*, and the *Santa Maria*

early 1492
queen of Spain agrees to help

Spain

Americas

## Time Line

| 1451 | around 1480 | 1484 | 1486 |
|------|-------------|------|------|
| born | makes voyages to sell cloth | first explains his idea to sail west to reach Asia | asks queen of Spain for help |

In 1492, Christopher and his crew sailed west from Spain. They landed on an island in the Americas after 71 days. Christopher thought they had landed in Asia. He made four trips to these islands.

early 1492
queen of Spain agrees to help;
October 1492
lands in the Americas

## Time Line

1451
born

around 1480
makes voyages
to sell cloth

1484
first explains his
idea to sail west
to reach Asia

1486
asks queen
of Spain
for help

20

Christopher never knew he had sailed to the Americas. He thought he had found a new course to Asia. He died in Spain in 1506. Christopher Columbus inspired many other sailors to explore the world.

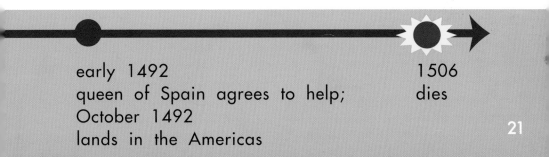

early 1492
queen of Spain agrees to help;
October 1492
lands in the Americas

1506
dies

# Words to Know

**Asia**—one of the seven continents of the world; countries in Asia include China, Japan, and India.

**chart**—a type of map; many charts are maps of stars or oceans.

**course**—a route or a plan for traveling

**crew**—a team of people who work together on a ship

**Europe**—one of the seven continents of the world; countries in Europe include England, France, and Spain.

**explore**—to travel to a new place to study it

**inspire**—to give someone the idea to do something

**queen**—a royal woman who rules her country

**trip**—a long journey; Christopher Columbus traveled more than 3,000 miles (4,800 kilometers) on his first trip to the Americas.

**weaver**—a person who makes cloth

# Read More

**Devillier, Christy.** *Christopher Columbus.* First Biographies. Edina, Minn.: Abdo, 2001.

**Kline, Trish.** *Christopher Columbus.* Discover the Life of an Explorer. Vero Beach, Fla.: Rourke, 2001.

**Larkin, Tanya.** *Christopher Columbus.* Famous Explorers. New York: PowerKids Press, 2001.

# Internet Sites

**Christopher Columbus: Explorer**
http://www.enchantedlearning.com/explorers/page/c/columbus.shtml

**Columbus Day: A History**
http://wilstar.com/holidays/columbus.htm

**The Explorations of Christopher Columbus**
http://www.mariner.org/age/columbus.html

**The Round Earth and Christopher Columbus**
http://www-istp.gsfc.nasa.gov/stargaze/Scolumb.htm

# Index/Word List

Word Count: 260
Early-Intervention Level: 24

**Editorial Credits**

Martha E. H. Rustad, editor; Heather Kindseth, cover designer and illustrator; Linda Clavel, illustrator; Kimberly Danger and Mary Englar, photo researchers

**Photo Credits**

North Wind Pictures, 1, 4, 10, 16, 20
Photri-Microstock, cover, 12
Stock Montage, 6, 8, 14